To My Husband and Other Poems

ANNE BRADSTREET

DOVER PUBLICATIONS, INC.
Mineola, New York

DOVER THRIFT EDITIONS

GENERAL EDITOR: PAUL NEGRI
EDITOR OF THIS VOLUME: ROBERT HUTCHINSON

Bibliographical Note

This Dover edition, first published in 2000, is a new selection of poems from *Poems of Anne Bradstreet*, edited by Robert Hutchinson, Dover Publications, Inc., Mineola, New York, 1969.

International Standard Book Number: 0-486-41408-6

Manufactured in the United States of America
Dover Publications, Inc., 31 East 2nd Street, Mineola, N.Y. 11501

Note

ANNE BRADSTREET (1612–1672) occupies a special place in American literary history as the author of the first published book of verse to be written in the New World. She was born in England, the child of Puritan parents in the employ of the earl of Lincoln, and educated by private tutors. At sixteen she married Simon Bradstreet, a Cambridge graduate, also in the employ of the earl of Lincoln, and in 1630, the Bradstreets, along with Anne's parents, emigrated to the Massachusetts Bay Colony. The Bradstreets prospered in the colony, Anne's father—and later her husband—serving as governors of Massachusetts.

Although the wife of a prosperous settler, Anne Bradstreet faced the same hardships and challenges that confronted all the early colonists. As the mother of eight children and the manager of the household, she had little time to pursue literary ambitions, which in themselves were considered unsuitable, and even harmful, in a Puritan colonial woman. But Bradstreet recognized the quality of her verse and persisted in writing it, making no attempt to publish it herself. It was her brother-in-law, John Woodbridge, who arranged, presumably without her knowledge, to have the *The Tenth Muse, Lately Sprung Up in America* printed in London in 1650. The book was an immediate success.

Bradstreet's best poems are those drawn from her personal experiences, where addressing her husband, children, and grandchildren, she gives voice to sincere and deep-felt sentiment in memorable verse that retains the power to move us. In her fine poem *Upon the Burning of Our House* , the grievousness of her loss and the courage of her acceptance of it epitomizes the strong yet sensitive nature from which her poetry sprung.

CONTENTS

III | *Religious Meditations*

The Author to her Book

Prehistory

Thou ill-form'd offspring of my feeble brain,
Who after birth did'st by my side remain,
Till snatcht from thence by friends, less wise than true
Who thee abroad, expos'd to publick view;
Made thee in raggs, halting to th' press to trudg,
Where errors were not lessened (all may judg)
At thy return my blushing was not small,
My rambling brat (in print) should mother call,
I cast thee by as one unfit for light,
Thy Visage was so irksome in my sight;   10
Yet being mine own, at length affection would
Thy blemishes amend, if so I could:
I wash'd thy face, but more defects I saw,
And rubbing off a spot, still made a flaw.
I stretcht thy joynts to make thee even feet,
Yet still thou run'st more hobling than is meet;
In better dress to trim thee was my mind,
But nought save home-spun Cloth, i'th' house I find.
In this array, 'mongst Vulgars mayst thou roam
In Criticks hands, beware thou dost not come;   20
And take thy way where yet thou art not known,
If for thy Father askt, say, thou hadst none:
And for thy Mother, she alas is poor,
Which caus'd her thus to send thee out of door.

WRITING is SOMETHING HISTORICAL

I / LOVE POEMS

To my Dear and loving Husband

If ever two were one, then surely we.
If ever man were lov'd by wife, then thee;
If ever wife was happy in a man,
Compare with me ye women if you can.
I prize thy love more than whole Mines of gold,
Or all the riches that the East doth hold.
My love is such that Rivers cannot quench,
Nor ought but love from thee, give recompence.
Thy love is such I can no way repay,
The heavens reward thee manifold I pray.　　10
Then while we live, in love lets so persever,
That when we live no more, we may live ever.

"As loving Hind"

As loving Hind that (Hartless) wants her Deer,
Scuds through the woods and Fern with harkning ear,
Perplext, in every bush and nook doth pry,
Her dearest Deer, might answer ear or eye;
So doth my anxious soul, which now doth miss,
A dearer Dear (far dearer Heart) than this,
Still wait with doubts, and hopes, and failing eye,
His voice to hear, or person to discry.
Or as the pensive Dove doth all alone
(On withered bough) most uncouthly bemoan　　10
The absence of her Love, and loving Mate,
Whose loss hath made her so unfortunate:

Ev'n thus doe I, with many a deep sad groan
Bewail my turtle true, who now is gone,
His presence and his safe return, still wooes,
With thousand dolefull sighs and mournfull Cooes.
Or as the loving Mullet, that true Fish,
Her fellow lost, nor joy nor life do wish,
But lanches on that shore, there for to dye,
Where she her captive husband doth espy.   20
Mine being gone, I lead a joyless life,
I have a loving phere, yet seem no wife:
But worst of all, to him can't steer my course,
I here, he there, alas, both kept by force:
Return my Dear, my joy, my only Love,
Unto thy Hinde, thy Mullet and thy Dove,
Who neither joyes in pasture, house nor streams,
The substance gone, O me, these are but dreams.
Together at one Tree, oh let us brouze,
And like two Turtles roost within one house,   30
And like the Mullets in one River glide,
Let's still remain but one, till death divide.

> { *Thy loving Love and Dearest Dear,*
> *At home, abroad, and every where.*

"Phœbus make haste"

Phœbus make haste, the day's too long, be gone,
The silent night's the fittest time for moan;
But stay this once, unto my suit give ear,
And tell my griefs in either Hemisphere:
(And if the whirling of thy wheels don't drown'd
The woful accents of my doleful sound),

If in thy swift Carrier thou canst make stay,
I crave this boon, this Errand by the way,
Commend me to the man more lov'd than life,
Shew him the sorrows of his widdowed wife;   10
My dumpish thoughts, my groans, my brakish tears
My sobs, my longing hopes, my doubting fears,
And if he love, how can he there abide?
My Interest's more than all the world beside.
He that can tell the starrs or Ocean sand,
Or all the grass that in the Meads do stand,
The leaves in th' woods, the hail or drops of rain,
Or in a corn-field number every grain,
Or every mote that in the sun-shine hops,
May count my sighs, and number all my drops: 20
Tell him, the countless steps that thou dost trace,
That once a day, thy Spouse thou mayst imbrace;
And when thou canst not treat by loving mouth,
Thy rayes afar, salute her from the south.
But for one moneth I see no day (poor soul)
Like those far scituate under the pole,
Which day by day long wait for thy arise,
O how they joy when thou dost light the skyes.
O *Phœbus*, hadst thou but thus long from thine
Restrain'd the beams of thy beloved shine,   30
At thy return, if so thou could'st or durst
Behold a Chaos blacker than the first.
Tell him here's worse than a confused matter,
His little world's a fathom under water,
Nought but the fervor of his ardent beams
Hath power to dry the torrent of these streams.
Tell him I would say more, but cannot well,
Oppressed minds, abruptest tales do tell.
Now post with double speed, mark what I say,
By all our loves conjure him not to stay.   40

A Letter to her Husband, absent upon Publick employment

My head, my heart, mine Eyes, my life, nay more,
My joy, my Magazine of earthly store,
If two be one, as surely thou and I,
How stayest thou there, whilst I at *Ipswich* lye?
So many steps, head from the heart to sever
If but a neck, soon should we be together:
I like the earth this season, mourn in black,
My Sun is gone so far in's Zodiack,
Whom whilst I 'joy'd, nor storms, nor frosts I felt,
His warmth such frigid colds did cause to melt.   10
My chilled limbs now nummed lye forlorn;
Return, return sweet *Sol* from *Capricorn*;
In this dead time, alas, what can I more
Than view those fruits which through thy heat I bore?
Which sweet contentment yield me for a space,
True living Pictures of their Fathers face.
O strange effect! now thou art *Southward* gone,
I weary grow, the tedious day so long;
But when thou *Northward* to me shalt return,
I wish my Sun may never set, but burn   20
Within the Cancer of my glowing breast,
The welcome house of him my dearest guest.
Where ever, ever stay, and go not thence,
Till natures sad decree shall call thee hence;
Flesh of thy flesh, bone of thy bone,
I here, thou there, yet both but one.

Before the Birth of one of her Children

All things within this fading world hath end,
Adversity doth still our joyes attend;
No tyes so strong, no friends so dear and sweet,
But with deaths parting blow is sure to meet.
The sentence past is most irrevocable,
A common thing, yet oh inevitable;
How soon, my Dear, death may my steps attend,
How soon't may be thy Lot to lose thy friend,
We both are ignorant, yet love bids me
These farewell lines to recommend to thee,   10
That when that knot's unty'd that made us one,
I may seem thine, who in effect am none.
And if I see not half my dayes that's due,
What nature would, God grant to yours and you;
The many faults that well you know I have,
Let be interr'd in my oblivious grave;
If any worth or virtue were in me,
Let that live freshly in thy memory
And when thou feel'st no grief, as I no harms,
Yet love thy dead, who long lay in thine arms: 20
And when thy loss shall be repaid with gains
Look to my little babes my dear remains.
And if thou love thy self, or loved'st me
These O protect from step Dames injury.
And if chance to thine eyes shall bring this verse,
With some sad sighs honour my absent Herse;
And kiss this paper for thy loves dear sake,
Who with salt tears this last Farewel did take.

II / DOMESTIC POEMS

In reference to her Children, 23. June, 1656

I had eight birds hatcht in one nest,
Four Cocks there were, and Hens the rest,
I nurst them up with pain and care,
Nor cost, nor labour did I spare,
Till at the last they felt their wing,
Mounted the Trees, and learn'd to sing;
Chief of the Brood then took his flight,
To Regions far, and left me quite:
My mournful chirps I after send,
Till he return, or I do end,   10
Leave not thy nest, thy Dam and Sire,
Fly back and sing amidst this Quire.
My second bird did take her flight,
And with her mate flew out of sight;
Southward they both their course did bend,
And Seasons twain they there did spend:
Till after blown by *Southern* gales,
They *Norward* steer'd with filled sayles.
A prettier bird was no where seen,
Along the Beach among the treen.   20
I have a third of colour white,
On whom I plac'd no small delight;
Coupled with mate loving and true,
Hath also bid her Dam adieu:
And where *Aurora* first appears,
She now hath percht, to spend her years;
One to the Academy flew
To chat among that learned crew:
Ambition moves still in his breast

That he might chant above the rest,   30
Striving for more than to do well,
That nightingales he might excell.
My fifth, whose down is yet scarce gone
Is 'mongst the shrubs and bushes flown,
And as his wings increase in strength,
On higher boughs he'l pearch at length.
My other three, still with me nest,
Untill they'r grown, then as the rest,
Or here or there, they'l take their flight,
As is ordain'd, so shall they light.   40
If birds could weep, then would my tears
Let others know what are my fears
Lest this my brood some harm should catch,
And be surpriz'd for want of watch,
Whilst pecking corn, and void of care
They fall un'wares in Fowlers snare:
Or whilst on trees they sit and sing,
Some untoward boy at them do fling:
Or whilst allur'd with bell and glass,
The net be spread, and caught, alas.   50
Or least by Lime-twigs they be foyl'd,
Or by some greedy hawks be spoyl'd.
O would my young, ye saw my breast,
And knew what thoughts there sadly rest,
Great was my pain when I you bred,
Great was my care, when I you fed,
Long did I keep you soft and warm,
And with my wings kept off all harm,
My cares are more, and fears than ever,
My throbs such now, as 'fore were never: 60
Alas my birds, you wisdome want,
Of perils you are ignorant,
Oft times in grass, on trees, in flight,

Sore accidents on you may light.
O to your safety have an eye,
So happy may you live and die:
Mean while my dayes in tunes Ile spend,
Till my weak layes with me shall end.
In shady woods I'le sit and sing,
And things that past, to mind I'le bring.   70
Once young and pleasant, as are you,
But former toyes (no joyes) adieu.
My age I will not once lament,
But sing, my time so near is spent.
And from the top bough take my flight,
Into a country beyond sight,
Where old ones, instantly grow young,
And there with Seraphims set song:
No seasons cold, nor storms they see;
But spring lasts to eternity,   80
When each of you shall in your nest
Among your young ones take your rest,
In chirping language, oft them tell,
You had a Dam that lov'd you well,
That did what could be done for young,
And nurst you up till you were strong,
And 'fore she once would let you fly,
She shew'd you joy and misery;
Taught what was good, and what was ill,
What would save life, and what would kill?   90
Thus gone, amongst you I may live,
And dead, yet speak, and counsel give:
Farewel my birds, farewel adieu,
I happy am, if well with you.

Upon a Fit of Sickness, Anno. 1632. Ætatis suæ, 19

Twice ten years old, not fully told
  Since nature gave me breath,
My race is run, my thread is spun,
  lo here is fatal Death.
All men must dye, and so must I
  this cannot be revok'd
For Adams sake, this word God spake
  when he so high provok'd.
Yet live I shall, this life's but small,
  in place of highest bliss,   10
Where I shall have all I can crave,
  no life is like to this.
For what's this life, but care and strife?
  since first we came from womb,
Our strength doth waste, our time doth hast,
  and then we go to th' Tomb.
O Bubble blast, how long can'st last?
  that always art a breaking,
No sooner blown, but dead and gone,
  ev'n as a word that's speaking.   20
O whil'st I live, this grace me give,
  I doing good may be,
Then deaths arrest I shall count best,
  because it's thy decree;
Bestow much cost there's nothing lost,
  to make Salvation sure,
O great's the gain, though got with pain,
  comes by profession pure.
The race is run, the field is won,
  the victory's mine I see,   30
For ever know, thou envious foe,
  the foyle belongs to thee.

To her Father with some verses

Most truly honoured, and as truly dear,
If worth in me, or ought I do appear,
Who can of right better demand the same?
Than may your worthy self from whom it came.
The principle might yield a greater sum,
Yet handled ill, amounts but to this crum;
My stock's so small, I know not how to pay,
My Bond remains in force unto this day;
Yet for part payment take this simple mite,
Where nothing's to be had Kings loose their right.   10
Such is my debt, I may not say forgive,
But as I can, I'le pay it while I live:
Such is my bond, none can discharge but I,
Yet paying is not payd until I dye.

To the Memory of my dear and ever honoured Father Thomas Dudley Esq; Who deceased, July 31. 1653. and of his Age, 77

By duty bound, and not by custome led,
To celebrate the praises of the dead,
My mournfull mind, sore prest, in trembling verse
Presents my Lamentations at his Herse,
Who was my Father, Guide, Instructer too,
To whom I ought whatever I could doe:
Nor is't Relation near my hand shall tye;
For who more cause to boast his worth than I?
Who heard or saw, observ'd or knew him better?
Or who alive than I, a greater debtor?   10
Let malice bite, and envy knaw its fill,
He was my Father, and Ile praise him still.

Nor was his name, or life lead so obscure
That pitty might some Trumpeters procure,
Who after death might make him falsly seem
Such as in life, no man could justly deem.
Well known and lov'd, where ere he liv'd, by most
Both in his native, and in foreign coast,
These to the world his merits could make known,
So needs no Testimonial from his own;   20
But now or never I must pay my Sum;
While others tell his worth, I'le not be dumb:
One of thy Founders, him *New-England* know,
Who staid thy feeble sides when thou wast low,
Who spent his state, his strength, and years with care
That After-comers in them might have share.
True Patriot of this little Commonweal,
Who is't can tax thee ought, but for thy zeal?
Truths friend thou wert, to errors still a foe,
Which caus'd Apostates to maligne so.   30
Thy love to true Religion e're shall shine,
My Fathers God, be God of me and mine.
Upon the earth he did not build his nest,
But as a Pilgrim, what he had, possest.
High thoughts he gave no harbour in his heart,
Nor honours pufft him up, when he had part:
Those titles loath'd, which some too much do love
For truly his ambition lay above.
His humble mind so lov'd humility,
He left it to his race for Legacy: 40
And oft and oft, with speeches mild and wise,
Gave his in charge, that Jewel rich to prize.
No ostentation seen in all his wayes,
As in the mean ones, of our foolish dayes,
Which all they have, and more still set to view,
Their greatness may be judg'd by what they shew.

His thoughts were more sublime, his actions wise,
Such vanityes he justly did despise.
Nor wonder 'twas, low things ne'r much did move
For he a Mansion had, prepar'd above, 50
For which he sigh'd and pray'd and long'd full sore
He might be cloath'd upon, for evermore.
Oft spake of death, and with a smiling chear,
He did exult his end was drawing near,
Now fully ripe, as shock of wheat that's grown,
Death as a Sickle hath him timely mown,
And in celestial Barn hath hous'd him high,
Where storms, nor showrs, nor ought can damnifie.
His Generation serv'd, his labours cease;
And to his Fathers gathered is in peace. 60
Ah happy Soul, 'mongst Saints and Angels blest,
Who after all his toyle, is now at rest:
His hoary head in righteousness was found:
As joy in heaven on earth let praise resound.
Forgotten never be his memory,
His blessing rest on his posterity:
His pious Footsteps followed by his race,
At last will bring us to that happy place
Where we with joy each others face shall see,
And parted more by death shall never be. 70

His Epitaph

Within this Tomb a Patriot lyes
That was both pious, just and wise,
To Truth a shield, to right a Wall,
To Sectaryes a whip and Maul,
A Magazine of History,
A Prizer of good Company

In manners pleasant and severe
The Good him lov'd, the bad did fear,
And when his time with years was spent
If some rejoyc'd, more did lament.　　　　　　80

An Epitaph On my dear and ever honoured Mother Mrs.
Dorothy Dudley, who deceased Decemb. 27. 1643. and
of her age, 61

> *Here lyes,*
> *A Worthy Matron of unspotted life,*
> *A loving Mother and obedient wife,*
> *A friendly Neighbor, pitiful to poor,*
> *Whom oft she fed, and clothed with her store;*
> *To Servants wisely aweful, but yet kind,*
> *And as they did, so they reward did find:*
> *A true Instructer of her Family,*
> *The which she ordered with dexterity.*
> *The publick meetings ever did frequent,*
> *And in her Closet constant hours she spent;*　　10
> *Religious in all her words and wayes,*
> *Preparing still for death, till end of dayes:*
> *Of all her Children, Children, liv'd to see,*
> *Then dying, left a blessed memory.*

Upon the burning of our house, July 10th, 1666

In silent night when rest I took,
For sorrow neer I did not look,
I waken'd was with thundring nois
And Piteous shreiks of dreadfull voice.
That fearfull sound of fire and fire,
Let no man know is my Desire.

I, starting up, the light did spye,
And to my God my heart did cry
To strengthen me in my Distresse
And not to leave me succourlesse.   10
Then coming out beheld a space,
The flame consume my dwelling place.

And, when I could no longer look,
I blest his Name that gave and took,
That layd my goods now in the dust:
Yea so it was, and so 'twas just.
It was his own: it was not mine;
Far be it that I should repine.

He might of All justly bereft,
But yet sufficient for us left.   20
When by the Ruines oft I past,
My sorrowing eyes aside did cast,
And here and there the places spye
Where oft I sate, and long did lye.

Here stood that Trunk, and there that chest;
There lay that store I counted best:
My pleasant things in ashes lye,
And them behold no more shall I.
Under thy roof no guest shall sitt,
Nor at thy Table eat a bitt.   30

No pleasant tale shall 'ere be told,
Nor things recounted done of old.
No Candle 'ere shall shine in Thee,
Nor bridegroom's voice ere heard shall bee.
In silence ever shalt thou lye;
Adeiu, Adeiu; All's vanity.

Then streight I gin my heart to chide,
And did thy wealth on earth abide?
Didst fix thy hope on mouldring dust,
The arm of flesh didst make thy trust?   40
Raise up thy thoughts above the skye
That dunghill mists away may flie.

Thou hast an house on high erect
Fram'd by that mighty Architect,
With glory richly furnished,
Stands permanent tho' this bee fled.
It's purchaséd, and paid for too
By him who hath enough to doe.

A Prise so vast as is unknown,
Yet, by his Gift, is made thine own.   50
Ther's wealth enough, I need no more;
Farewell my Pelf, farewell my Store.
The world no longer let me Love,
My hope and Treasure lyes Above.

Upon some distemper of body

In anguish of my heart repleat with woes,
And wasting pains, which best my body knows,
In tossing slumbers on my wakeful bed,
Bedrencht with tears that flow'd from mournful head,
Till nature had exhausted all her store,
Then eyes lay dry, disabled to weep more;
And looking up unto his Throne on high,
Who sendeth help to those in misery;
He chac'd away those clouds, and let me see
My Anchor cast i'th' vale with safety.   10
He eas'd my Soul of woe, my flesh of pain,
And brought me to the shore from troubled Main.

*In memory of my dear grand-child Elizabeth Bradstreet,
who deceased August, 1665. being a year and a half old*

Farewel dear babe, my hearts too much content,
Farewel sweet babe, the pleasure of mine eye,
Farewel fair flower that for a space was lent,
Then ta'en away unto Eternity.
Blest babe why should I once bewail thy fate,
Or sigh thy dayes so soon were terminate;
Sith thou art setled in an Everlasting state.

2

By nature Trees do rot when they are grown.
And Plumbs and Apples throughly ripe do fall,
And Corn and grass are in their season mown,   10
And time brings down what is both strong and tall.
But plants new set to be eradicate,
And buds new blown, to have so short a date,
Is by his hand alone that guides nature and fate.

*In memory of my dear grand-child Anne Bradstreet.
Who deceased June 20. 1669. being three years and seven
Moneths old*

With troubled heart and trembling hand I write,
The Heavens have chang'd to sorrow my delight.
How oft with disappointment have I met,
When I on fading things my hopes have set?
Experience might 'fore this have made me wise,
To value things according to their price:
Was ever stable joy yet found below,
Or perfect bliss without mixture of woe?

I knew she was but as a withering flour,
That's here to day, perhaps gone in an hour;   10
Like as a bubble, or the brittle glass,
Or like a shadow turning as it was.
More fool then I to look on that was lent,
As if mine own, when thus impermanent.
Farewel dear child, thou ne're shall come to me,
But yet a while, and I shall go to thee;
Mean time my throbbing heart's chear'd up with this
Thou with thy Saviour art in endless bliss.

*On my dear Grand-child Simon Bradstreet, Who dyed
on 16. Novemb. 1669. being but a moneth, and one day
old*

No sooner come, but gone, and fal'n asleep,
Acquaintance short, yet parting caus'd us weep,
Three flours, two scarcely blown, the last i'th' bud,
Cropt by th' Almighties hand; yet is he good,
With dreadful awe before him let's be mute,
Such was his will, but why, let's not dispute,
With humble hearts and mouths put in the dust,
Let's say he's merciful as well as just.
He will return, and make up all our losses,
And smile again, after our bitter crosses.   10
Go pretty babe, go rest with Sisters twain
Among the blest in endless joyes remain.

*To the memory of my dear Daughter in Law, Mrs.
Mercy Bradstreet, who deceased Sept. 6. 1669. in the
28. year of her Age*

And live I still to see Relations gone,
And yet survive to sound this wailing tone;

Ah, woe is me, to write thy Funeral Song,
Who might in reason yet have lived long,
I saw the branches lopt the Tree now fall,
I stood so nigh, it crusht me down withal;
My bruised heart lies sobbing at the Root,
That thou dear Son hath lost both Tree and fruit:
Thou then on Seas sailing to forreign Coast;
Was ignorant what riches thou hadst lost.   10
But ah too soon those heavy tydings fly,
To strike thee with amazing misery;
Oh how I simpathize with thy sad heart,
And in thy griefs still bear a second part:
I lost a daughter dear, but thou a wife,
Who lov'd thee more (it seem'd) than her own life.
Thou being gone, she longer could not be,
Because her Soul she'd sent along with thee.
One week she only past in pain and woe,
And then her sorrows all at once did go;   20
A Babe she left before, she soar'd above,
The fifth and last pledg of her dying love,
E're nature would, it hither did arrive,
No wonder it no longer did survive.
So with her Children four, she's now a rest,
All freed from grief (I trust) among the blest;
She one hath left, a joy to thee and me,
The Heavens vouchsafe she may so ever be.
Chear up, (dear Son) thy fainting bleeding heart,
In him alone, that caused all this smart;   30
What though thy strokes full sad and grievous be,
He knows it is the best for thee and me.

III / RELIGIOUS MEDITATIONS

To my Dear Children

This book by Any yet unread,
I leave for you when I am dead,
That, being gone, here you may find
What was your liveing mother's mind.
Make use of what I leave in Love
And God shall blesse you from above.

A Journal or notes written for her children

"By night when others soundly slept"

I

By night when others soundly slept,
And had at once both ease and Rest,
My waking eyes were open kept,
And so to lye I found it best.

II

I sought him whom my Soul did Love,
With tears I sought him earnestly;
He bow'd his ear down from Above,
In vain I did not seek or cry.

III

My hungry Soul he fill'd with Good,
He in his Bottle putt my teares,   10
My smarting wounds washt in his blood,
And banisht thence my Doubts and feares.

What to my Saviour shall I give,
Who freely hath done this for me?
I'le serve him here whilst I shall live,
And Love him to Eternity.

For Deliverance from a feaver

When Sorrowes had begyrt me round,
  And Paines within and out,
When in my flesh no part was found,
  Then didst thou rid me out.

My burning flesh in sweat did boyle,
  My aking head did break;
From side to side for ease I toyle,
  So faint I could not speak.

Beclouded was my Soul with fear
  Of thy Displeasure sore,   10
Nor could I read my Evidence
  Which oft I read before.

Hide not thy face from me, I cry'd,
  From Burnings keep my soul;
Thou know'st my heart, and hast me try'd;
  I on thy Mercyes Rowl.

O, heal my Soul, thou know'st I said,
  Tho' flesh consume to nought;
What tho' in dust it shall bee lay'd,
  To Glory shall bee brought.   20

Thou heardst, thy rod thou didst remove,
  And spar'd my Body frail,
Thou shew'st to me thy tender Love,
  My heart no more might quail.

O, Praises to my mighty God,
  Praise to my Lord, I say,
Who hath redeem'd my Soul from pitt:
  Praises to him for Aye!

From another sore Fitt

In my distresse I sought the Lord,
When nought on Earth could comfort give;
And when my Soul these things abhor'd,
Then, Lord, thou said'st unto me, Live.

Thou knowest the sorrowes that I felt,
My plaints and Groanes were heard of Thee,
And how in sweat I seem'd to melt;
Thou help'st and thou regardest me.

My wasted flesh thou didst restore,
My feeble loines didst gird with strenght;   10
Yea, when I was most low and poor,
I said I shall praise thee at lenght.

What shall I render to my God
For all his Bounty shew'd to me,
Even for his mercyes in his rod,
Where pitty most of all I see?

My heart I wholly give to Thee:
O make it fruitfull, faithfull Lord!
My life shall dedicated bee
To praise in thought, in Deed, in Word.   20

Thou know'st no life I did require
Longer than still thy Name to praise,
Nor ought on Earth worthy Desire,
In drawing out these wretched Dayes.

Thy Name and praise to celebrate,
O Lord! for aye is my request.
O, graunt I doe it in this state,
And then with thee which is the Best.

Deliverance from a fitt of Fainting

Worthy art Thou, O Lord of praise!
    But ah! it's not in me;
My sinking heart I pray thee raise,
    So shall I give it Thee.

My life as Spider's webb's cutt off,
    Thus fainting have I said,
And liveing man no more shall see,
    But bee in silence layd.

My feblee Spirit thou didst revive,
    My Doubting thou didst chide,   10
And tho' as dead mad'st me alive,
    I here a while might 'bide.

Why should I live but to thy Praise?
    My life is hid with Thee;
O Lord, no longer bee my Dayes,
    Than I may fruitfull bee.

"*What God is like to him I serve*"

What God is like to him I serve,
  What Saviour like to mine?
O, never let me from thee swerve,
  For truly I am thine.

My thankfull mouth shall speak thy praise,
  My Tongue shall talk of Thee:
On High my heart, O, doe thou raise,
  For what thou'st done for me.

Goe, Worldlings, to your Vanities,
  And heathen to your Gods;   10
Let them help in Adversities,
  And sanctefye their rods.

My God he is not like to yours,
  Your selves shall Judges bee;
I find his Love, I know his Pow'r,
  A Succourer of mee.

He is not man that he should lye,
  Nor son of man to unsay;
His word he plighted hath on high,
  And I shall live for aye.   20

And for his sake that faithfull is,
  That dy'd but now doth live,
The first and last, that lives for aye,
  Me lasting life shall give.

"*My soul, rejoice thou in thy God*"

My soul, rejoice thou in thy God,
    Boast of him all the Day,
Walk in his Law, and kisse his Rod,
    Cleave close to him alway.

What tho' thy outward Man decay,
    Thy inward shall waxe strong;
Thy body vile it shall bee chang'd,
    And glorious made ere-long.

With Angels-wings thy Soul shall mount
    To Blisse unseen by Eye,   10
And drink at unexhausted fount
    Of Joy unto Eternity.

Thy teares shall All bee dryed up,
    Thy Sorrowes all shall flye;
Thy Sinns shall ne'er bee summon'd up,
    Nor come in memory.

Then shall I know what thou hast done
    For me, unworthy me,
And praise thee shall ev'n as I ought,
    For wonders that I see.   20

Base World, I trample on thy face,
    Thy Glory I despise,
No gain I find in ought below,
    For God hath made me wise.

Come, Jesus, quickly, Blessed Lord,
    Thy face when shall I see?
O let me count each hour a Day
    'Till I dissolved bee.

"*As spring the winter doth succeed*"

As spring the winter doth succeed,
And leaves the naked Trees doe dresse,
The earth all black is cloth'd in green;
At sun-shine each their joy expresse.

My Suns returned with healing wings,
My Soul and Body doth rejoice;
My heart exults, and praises sings
To him that heard my wailing Voice.

My winters past, my stormes are gone,
And former clowdes seem now all fled;   10
But, if they must eclipse again,
I'le run where I was succoured.

I have a shelter from the storm,
A shadow from the fainting heat;
I have accesse unto his Throne,
Who is a God so wondrous great.

O hast thou made my Pilgrimage
Thus pleasant, fair, and good;
Bless'd me in Youth and elder Age,
My Baca made a springing flood?   20

I studious am what I shall doe,
To show my Duty with delight;
All I can give is but thine own,
And at the most a simple mite.

Upon my Son Samuel his goeing for England, Novem. 6, 1657

Thou mighty God of Sea and Land,
I here resigne into thy hand
The Son of Prayers, of vowes, of teares,
The child I stay'd for many yeares.
Thou heard'st me then, and gav'st him me;
Hear me again, I give him Thee.
He's mine, but more, O Lord, thine own,
For sure thy Grace on him is shown.
No freind I have like Thee to trust,
For mortall helpes are brittle Dust.   10
Preserve, O Lord, from stormes and wrack,
Protect him there, and bring him back;
And if thou shalt spare me a space,
That I again may see his face,
Then shall I celebrate thy Praise,
And Blesse thee for't even all my Dayes.
If otherwise I goe to Rest,
Thy Will bee done, for that is best;
Persuade my heart I shall him see
For ever happefy'd with Thee.   20

"My thankfull heart with glorying Tongue"

My thankfull heart with glorying Tongue
   Shall celebrate thy Name,
Who hath restor'd, redeem'd, recur'd
   From sicknes, death, and Pain.

I cry'd thou seem'st to make some stay,
   I sought more earnestly;
And in due time thou succour'st me,
   And sent'st me help from High.

Lord, whilst my fleeting time shall last,
   Thy Goodnes let me Tell.   10
And new Experience I have gain'd,
   My future Doubts repell.

An humble, faitefull life, O Lord,
   For ever let me walk;
Let my obedience testefye,
   My Praise lyes not in Talk.

Accept, O Lord, my simple mite,
   For more I cannot give;
What thou bestow'st I shall restore,
   For of thine Almes I live.   20

*For the restoration of my dear Husband from a burning
Ague, June, 1661*

When feares and sorrowes me besett,
   Then did'st thou rid me out;
When heart did faint and spirits quail,
   Thou comforts me about.

Thou rais'st him up I feard to loose,
   Regav'st me him again:
Distempers thou didst chase away;
   With strenght didst him sustain.

My thankfull heart, with Pen record
   The Goodnes of thy God;   10
Let thy obedience testefye
   He taught thee by his rod.

And with his staffe did thee support,
    That thou by both may'st learn;
And 'twixt the good and evill way,
    At last, thou mig'st discern.

Praises to him who hath not left
    My Soul as destitute;
Nor turnd his ear away from me,
    But graunted hath my Suit.   20

Upon my Daughter Hannah Wiggin her recovery from a dangerous feaver

Bles't bee thy Name, who did'st restore
    To health my Daughter dear
When death did seem ev'n to approach,
    And life was ended near.

Graunt shee remember what thou'st done,
    And celebrate thy Praise;
And let her Conversation say,
    Shee loves thee all thy Dayes.

On my Sons Return out of England, July 17, 1661

All Praise to him who hath now turn'd
My feares to Joyes, my sighes to song,
My Teares to smiles, my sad to glad:
He's come for whom I waited long.

Thou di'st preserve him as he went;
In raging stormes did'st safely keep:
Did'st that ship bring to quiet Port.
The other sank low in the Deep.

From Dangers great thou did'st him free
Of Pyrates who were neer at hand;   10
And order'st so the adverse wind,
That he before them gott to Land.

In country strange thou did'st provide,
And freinds rais'd him in every Place;
And courtesies of sundry sorts
From such as 'fore nere saw his face.

In sicknes when he lay full sore,
His help and his Physitian wer't;
When royall ones that Time did dye,
Thou heal'dst his flesh, and cheer'd his heart.   20

From troubles and Incūbers Thou,
(Without all fraud), did'st sett him free,
That, without scandall, he might come
To th' Land of his Nativity.

On Eagles wings him hether brought
Thro' Want and Dangers manifold;
And thus hath graunted my Request,
That I thy Mercyes might behold.

O help me pay my Vowes, O Lord!
That ever I may thankfull bee,   30
And may putt him in mind of what
Tho'st done for him, and so for me.

In both our hearts erect a frame
Of Duty and of Thankfullnes,
That all thy favours great receiv'd,
Oure upright walking may expresse.

Upon my dear and loving husband his goeing into England, Jan. 16, 1661

O Thou most high who rulest All,
    And hear'st the Prayers of Thine;
O hearken, Lord, unto my suit,
    And my Petition signe.

Into thy everlasting Armes
    Of mercy I commend
Thy servant, Lord. Keep and preserve
    My husband, my dear freind.

At thy command, O Lord, he went,
    Nor nought could keep him back;   10
Then let thy promis joy his heart:
    O help, and bee not slack.

Upon my heart in Thee, O God,
    Thou art my strenght and stay;
Thou see'st how weak and frail I am,
    Hide not thy face Away.

I, in obedience to thy Will,
    Thou knowest, did submitt;
It was my Duty so to doe,
    O Lord, accept of it.   20

Unthankfullnes for mercyes Past,
    Impute thou not to me;
O Lord, thou know'st my weak desire
    Was to sing Praise to Thee.

Lord, bee thou Pilott to the ship,
   And send them prosperous gailes;
In stormes and sicknes, Lord, preserve.
   Thy Goodnes never failes.

Unto thy work he hath in hand,
   Lord, graunt Thou good Successe   30
And favour in their eyes, to whom
   He shall make his Addresse.

Remember, Lord, thy folk whom thou
   To wildernesse hast brought;
Let not thine own Inheritance
   Bee sold away for Nought.

But Tokens of thy favour Give—
   With Joy send back my Dear,
That I, and all thy servants, may
   Rejoice with heavenly chear.   40

Lord, let my eyes see once Again
   Him whom thou gavest me,
That wee together may sing Praise
   For ever unto Thee.

And the Remainder of oure Dayes
   Shall consecrated bee,
With an engaged heart to sing
   All Praises unto Thee.

In my Solitary houres in my dear husband his Absence

O Lord, thou hear'st my dayly moan,
    And see'st my dropping teares:
My Troubles All are Thee before,
    My Longings and my feares.

Thou hetherto hast been my God;
    Thy help my soul hath found:
Tho' losse and sicknes me assail'd,
    Thro' thee I've kept my Ground.

And thy Abode tho'st made with me;
    With Thee my Soul can talk   10
In secrett places, Thee I find,
    Where I doe kneel or walk.

Tho' husband dear bee from me gone,
    Whom I doe love so well;
I have a more beloved one
    Whose comforts far excell.

O stay my heart on thee, my God,
    Uphold my fainting Soul!
And, when I know not what to doe,
    I'll on thy mercyes roll.   20

My weaknes, thou do'st know full well,
    Of Body and of mind.
I, in this world, no comfort have,
    But what from Thee I find.

Tho' children thou hast given me,
    And freinds I have also:
Yet, if I see Thee not thro' them,
    They are no Joy, but woe.

O shine upon me, blessed Lord,
   Ev'n for my Saviour's sake;   30
In Thee Alone is more than All,
   And there content I'll take.

O hear me, Lord, in this Request,
   As thou before ha'st done:
Bring back my husband, I beseech,
   As thou didst once my Sonne.

So shall I celebrate thy Praise,
   Ev'n while my Dayes shall last;
And talk to my Beloved one
   Of all thy Goodnes past.   40

So both of us thy Kindnes, Lord,
   With Praises shall recount,
And serve Thee better than before,
   Whose Blessings thus surmount.

But give me, Lord, a better heart,
   Then better shall I bee,
To pay the vowes which I doe owe
   For ever unto Thee.

Unlesse thou help, what can I doe
   But still my frailty show?   50
If thou assist me, Lord, I shall
   Return Thee what I owe.

In thankfull acknowledgment for the letters I received from my husband out of England

O Thou that hear'st the Prayers of Thine,
And 'mongst them hast regarded Mine,
Hast heard my cry's, and seen my Teares;
Hast known my doubts and All my Feares.

Thou hast releiv'd my fainting heart,
Nor payd me after my desert;
Thou hast to shore him safely brought
For whom I thee so oft besought.

Thou wast the Pilott to the ship,
And rais'd him up when he was sick;   10
And hope thou'st given of good successe,
In this his Buisnes and Addresse;

And that thou wilt return him back,
Whose presence I so much doe lack.
For All these mercyes I thee Praise,
And so desire ev'n all my Dayes.

In thankfull Remembrance for my dear husbands safe Arrivall Sept. 3, 1662

What shall I render to thy Name,
   Or how thy Praises speak;
My thankes how shall I testefye?
   O Lord, thou know'st I'm weak.

I ow so much, so little can
   Return unto thy Name,
Confusion seases on my Soul,
   And I am fill'd with shame.

O thou that hearest Prayers, Lord,
  To Thee shall come all Flesh;   10
Thou hast me heard and answered,
  My 'Plaints have had accesse.

What did I ask for but thou gav'st?
  What could I more desire?
But Thankfullnes, even all my dayes,
  I humbly this Require.

Thy mercyes, Lord, have been so great,
  In number numberles,
Impossible for to recount
  Or any way expresse.   20

O help thy Saints that sought thy Face,
  T' Return unto thee Praise,
And walk before thee as they ought,
  In strict and upright wayes.

"*As weary pilgrim, now at rest*"

As weary pilgrim, now at rest,
  Hugs with delight his silent nest
His wasted limbes, now lye full soft
  That myrie steps, have troden oft
Blesses himself, to think upon
  his dangers past, and travailes done
The burning sun no more shall heat
  Nor stormy raines, on him shall beat.
The bryars and thornes no more shall scratch
  nor hungry wolves at him shall catch   10

He erring pathes no more shall tread
   nor wild fruits eate, in stead of bread,
for waters cold he doth not long
   for thirst no more shall parch his tongue
No rugged stones his feet shall gaule
   nor stumps nor rocks cause him to fall
All cares and feares, he bids farwell
   and meanes in safity now to dwell.
A pilgrim I, on earth, perplext
   with sinns with cares and sorrows vext   20
By age and paines brought to decay
   and my Clay house mouldring away
Oh how I long to be at rest
   and soare on high among the blest.
This body shall in silence sleep
   Mine eyes no more shall ever weep
No fainting fits shall me assaile
   nor grinding paines my body fraile
With cares and fears ne'r cumbred be
   Nor losses know, nor sorrowes see   30
What tho my flesh shall there consume
   it is the bed Christ did perfume
And when a few yeares shall be gone
   this mortall shall be cloth'd upon
A Corrupt Carcasse downe it lyes
   a glorious body it shall rise
In weaknes and dishonour sowne
   in power 'tis rais'd by Christ alone
Then soule and body shall unite
   and of their maker have the sight   40
Such lasting joyes shall there behold
   as eare ne'r heard nor tongue e'er told
Lord make me ready for that day
   then Come deare bridgrome Come away.

IV / CONTEMPLATIONS

1

Some time now past in the Autumnal Tide,
When *Phœbus* wanted but one hour to bed,
The trees all richly clad, yet void of pride,
Where gilded o're by his rich golden head.
Their leaves and fruits seem'd painted, but was true
Of green, of red, of yellow, mixed hew,
Rapt were my sences at this delectable view.

2

I wist not what to wish, yet sure thought I,
If so much excellence abide below;
How excellent is he that dwells on high?
Whose power and beauty by his works we know.
Sure he is goodness, wisdome, glory, light,
That hath this under world so richly dight: 13
More Heaven than Earth was here no winter and no
            night.

3

Then on a stately Oak I cast mine Eye,
Whose ruffling top the Clouds seem'd to aspire;
How long since thou wast in thine Infancy?
Thy strength, and stature, more thy years admire,
Hath hundred winters past since thou wast born?
Or thousand since thou brakest thy shell of horn,
If so, all these as nought, Eternity doth scorn.

4

Then higher on the glistering Sun I gaz'd,
Whose beams was shaded by the leavie Tree,
The more I look'd, the more I grew amaz'd,
And softly said, what glory's like to thee?
Soul of this world, this Universes Eye,
No wonder, some made thee a Deity:
Had I not better known, (alas) the same had I.   28

5

Thou as a Bridegroom from thy Chamber rushes,
And as a strong man, joyes to run a race,
The morn doth usher thee, with smiles and blushes,
The Earth reflects her glances in thy face.
Birds, insects, Animals with Vegative,
Thy heat from death and dulness doth revive:
And in the darksome womb of fruitful nature dive.

6

Thy swift Annual, and diurnal Course,
Thy daily streight, and yearly oblique path,
Thy pleasing fervor, and thy scorching force,
All mortals here the feeling knowledg hath.
Thy presence makes it day, thy absence night,
Quaternal Seasons caused by thy might:
Hail Creature, full of sweetness, beauty and delight.   42

7

Art thou so full of glory, that no Eye
Hath strength, thy shining Rayes once to behold?
And is thy splendid Throne erect so high?
As to approach it, can no earthly mould.
How full of glory then must thy Creator be?
Who gave this bright light luster unto thee:
Admir'd, ador'd for ever, be that Majesty.

8

Silent alone, where none or saw, or heard,
In pathless paths I lead my wandring feet,
My humble Eyes to lofty Skyes I rear'd
To sing some Song, my mazed Muse thought meet.
My great Creator I would magnifie,
That nature had, thus decked liberally:
But Ah, and Ah, again, my imbecility!   56

9

I heard the merry grashopper then sing,
The black clad Cricket, bear a second part,
They kept one tune, and plaid on the same string,
Seeming to glory in their little Art.
Shall Creatures abject, thus their voices raise?
And in their kind resound their makers praise:
Whilst I as mute, can warble forth no higher layes.

10

When present times look back to Ages past,
And men in being fancy those are dead,
It makes things gone perpetually to last,
And calls back moneths and years that long since fled
It makes a man more aged in conceit,
Than was *Methuselah*, or's grand-sire great: 69
While of their persons and their acts his mind doth treat.

11

Sometimes in *Eden* fair, he seems to be,
Sees glorious *Adam* there made Lord of all,
Fancyes the Apple, dangle on the Tree,
That turn'd his Sovereign to a naked thral.
Who like a miscreant's driven from that place,
To get his bread with pain, and sweat of face:
A penalty impos'd on his backsliding Race.

12

Here sits our Grandame in retired place,
And in her lap, her bloody *Cain* new born,
The weeping Imp oft looks her in the face,
Bewails his unknown hap, and fate forlorn;
His Mother sighs, to think of Paradise,
And how she lost her bliss, to be more wise,
Believing him that was, and is, Father of lyes.   84

13

Here *Cain* and *Abel* come to sacrifice,
Fruits of the Earth, and Fatlings each do bring,
On *Abels* gift the fire descends from Skies,
But no such sign on false *Cain's* offering;
With sullen hateful looks he goes his wayes.
Hath thousand thoughts to end his brothers dayes,
Upon whose blood his future good he hopes to raise.

14

There *Abel* keeps his sheep, no ill he thinks,
His brother comes, then acts his fratricide,
The Virgin Earth, of blood her first draught drinks
But since that time she often hath been cloy'd;
The wretch with gastly face and dreadful mind,
Thinks each he sees will serve him in his kind,   97
Though none on Earth but kindred near then could he
          find.

15

Who fancyes not his looks now at the Barr,
His face like death, his heart with horror fraught,
Nor Male-factor ever felt like warr,
When deep dispair, with wish of life hath fought,
Branded with guilt, and crusht with treble woes,
A Vagabond to Land of *Nod* he goes.
A City builds, that wals might him secure from foes.

16

Who thinks not oft upon the Fathers ages.
Their long descent, how nephews sons they saw,
The starry observations of those Sages,
And how their precepts to their sons were law,
How Adam sigh'd to see his Progeny,
Cloath'd all in his black sinfull Livery,
Who neither guilt, nor yet the punishment could fly. 112

17

Our Life compare we with their length of dayes
Who to the tenth of theirs doth now arrive?
And though thus short, we shorten many wayes,
Living so little while we are alive;
In eating, drinking, sleeping, vain delight
So unawares comes on perpetual night,
And puts all pleasures vain unto eternal flight.

18

When I behold the heavens as in their prime,
And then the earth (though old) stil clad in green,
The stones and trees, insensible of time,
Nor age nor wrinkle on their front are seen;
If winter come, and greeness then do fade,
A Spring returns, and they more youthfull made; 125
But Man grows old, lies down, remains where once he's
        laid.

19

By birth more noble than those creatures all,
Yet seems by nature and by custome curs'd,
No sooner born, but grief and care makes fall
That state obliterate he had at first:
Nor youth, nor strength, nor wisdom spring again
Nor habitations long their names retain,
But in oblivion to the final day remain.

20

Shall I then praise the heavens, the trees, the earth
Because their beauty and their strength last longer
Shall I wish there, or never to had birth,
Because they're bigger, and their bodyes stronger?
Nay, they shall darken, perish, fade and dye,
And when unmade, so ever shall they lye,
But man was made for endless immortality.   140

21

Under the cooling shadow of a stately Elm
Close sate I by a goodly Rivers side,
Where gliding streams the Rocks did overwhelm;
A lonely place, with pleasures dignifi'd.
I once that lov'd the shady woods so well,
Now thought the rivers did the trees excel,
And if the sun would ever shine, there would I dwell.

22

While on the stealing stream I fixt mine eye,
Which to the long'd for Ocean held its course,
I markt, nor crooks, nor rubs that there did lye
Could hinder ought, but still augment its force:
O happy Flood, quoth I, that holds thy race
Till thou arrive at thy beloved place,
Nor is it rocks or shoals that can obstruct thy pace.   154

23

Nor is't enough, that thou alone may'st slide,
But hundred brooks in thy cleer waves do meet,
So hand in hand along with thee they glide
To *Thetis* house, where all imbrace and greet:
Thou Emblem true, of what I count the best,
O could I lead my Rivolets to rest,
So may we press to that vast mansion, ever blest.

24

Ye Fish which in this liquid Region 'bide,
That for each season, have your habitation,
Now salt, now fresh where you think best to glide
To unknown coasts to give a visitation,
In Lakes and ponds, you leave your numerous fry,
So nature taught, and yet you know not why,
You watry folk that know not your felicity.   168

25

Look how the wantons frisk to tast the air,
Then to the colder bottome streight they dive,
Eftsoon to *Neptun's* glassie Hall repair
To see what trade they great ones there do drive,
Who forrage o're the spacious sea-green field,
And take the trembling prey before it yield,
Whose armour is their scales, their spreading fins their
        shield.

26

While musing thus with contemplation fed,
And thousand fancies buzzing in my brain,
The sweet-tongu'd Philomel percht ore my head,
And chanted forth a most melodious strain
Which rapt me so with wonder and delight,
I judg'd my hearing better than my sight,   181
And wisht me wings with her a while to take my flight.

27

O merry Bird (said I) that fears no snares,
That neither toyles nor hoards up in thy barn,
Feels no sad thoughts, nor cruciating cares
To gain more good, or shun what might thee harm
Thy cloaths ne're wear, thy meat is every where,
Thy bed a bough, thy drink the water cleer,
Reminds not what is past, nor whats to come dost fear.

28

The dawning morn with songs thou dost prevent,
Sets hundred notes unto thy feathered crew,
So each one tunes his pretty instrument,
And warbling out the old, begin anew,
And thus they pass their youth in summer season,
Then follow thee into a better Region,
where winter's never felt by that sweet airy legion.   196

29

Man at the best a creature frail and vain,
In knowledg ignorant, in strength but weak,
Subject to sorrows, losses, sickness, pain,
Each storm his state, his mind, his body break,
From some of these he never finds cessation,
But day or night, within, without, vexation,
Troubles from foes, from friends, from dearest, near'st
Relation.

30

And yet this sinfull creature, frail and vain,
This lump of wretchedness, of sin and sorrow,
This weather-beaten vessel wrackt with pain,
Joyes not in hope of an eternal morrow;
Nor all his losses, crosses and vexation,
In weight, in frequency and long duration   209
Can make him deeply groan for that divine Translation.

31

The Mariner that on smooth waves doth glide,
Sings merrily, and steers his Barque with ease,
As if he had command of wind and tide,
And now become great Master of the seas;
But suddenly a storm spoiles all the sport,
And makes him long for a more quiet port,
Which 'gainst all adverse winds may serve for fort.

32

So he that saileth in this world of pleasure,
Feeding on sweets, that never bit of th' sowre,
That's full of friends, of honour and of treasure,
Fond fool, he takes this earth ev'n for heav'ns bower.
But sad affliction comes and makes him see
Here's neither honour, wealth, nor safety;
Only above is found all with security.   224

33

O Time the fatal wrack of mortal things,
That draws oblivions curtains over kings,
Their sumptuous monuments, men know them not,
Their names without a Record are forgot,
Their parts, their ports, their pomp's all laid in th' dust
Nor wit nor gold, nor buildings scape times rust;
But he whose name is grav'd in the white stone
Shall last and shine when all of these are gone.

V / DIALOGUES AND
LAMENTATIONS

The Flesh and the Spirit

In secret place where once I stood
Close by the Banks of *Lacrim* flood
I heard two sisters reason on
Things that are past, and things to come;
One flesh was call'd, who had her eye
On worldly wealth and vanity;
The other Spirit, who did rear
Her thoughts unto a higher sphere:
Sister, quoth Flesh, what liv'st thou on
Nothing but Meditation?   10
Doth Contemplation feed thee so
Regardlesly to let earth goe?
Can Speculation satisfy
Notion without Reality?
Dost dream of things beyond the Moon
And dost thou hope to dwell there soon?
Hast treasures there laid up in store
That all in th' world thou count'st but poor?
Art fancy sick, or turn'd a Sot
To catch at shadowes which are not?   20
Come, come, Ile shew unto thy sence,
Industry hath its recompence.
What canst desire, but thou maist see
True substance in variety?
Dost honour like? acquire the same,
As some to their immortal fame:
And trophyes to thy name erect
Which wearing time shall ne're deject.

For riches dost thou long full sore?
Behold enough of precious store.   30
Earth hath more silver, pearls and gold,
Than eyes can see, or hands can hold.
Affect's thou pleasure? take thy fill,
Earth hath enough of what you will.
Then let not goe, what thou maist find,
For things unknown, only in mind.
Spir. Be still thou unregenerate part,
Disturb no more my setled heart,
For I have vow'd, (and so will doe)
Thee as a foe, still to pursue.   40
And combate with thee will and must,
Untill I see thee laid in th' dust.
Sisters we are, ye twins we be,
Yet deadly feud 'twixt thee and me;
For from one father are we not,
Thou by old Adam wast begot,
But my arise is from above,
Whence my dear father I do love.
Thou speak'st me fair, but hat'st me sore,
Thy flatt'ring shews Ile trust no more.   50
How oft thy slave, hast thou me made,
when I believ'd, what thou hast said,
And never had more cause of woe
Than when I did what thou bad'st doe.
Ile stop mine ears at these thy charms,
And count them for my deadly harms.
Thy sinfull pleasures I doe hate,
Thy riches are to me no bait,
Thine honours doe, nor will I love;
For my ambition lyes above.   60
My greatest honour it shall be
When I am victor over thee,

And triumph shall, with laurel head,
When thou my Captive shalt be led,
How I do live, thou need'st not scoff,
For I have meat thou know'st not off;
The hidden Manna I doe eat,
The word of life it is my meat.
My thoughts do yield me more content
Than can thy hours in pleasure spent.   70
Nor are they shadows which I catch,
Nor fancies vain at which I snatch,
But reach at things that are so high,
Beyond thy dull Capacity;
Eternal substance I do see,
With which inriched I would be:
Mine Eye doth pierce the heavens, and see
What is Invisible to thee.
My garments are not silk nor gold,
Nor such like trash which Earth doth hold,   80
But Royal Robes I shall have on,
More glorious than the glistring Sun;
My Crown not Diamonds, Pearls, and gold,
But such as Angels heads infold.
The City where I hope to dwell,
There's none on Earth can parallel;
The stately Walls both high and strong,
Are made of pretious *Jasper* stone;
The Gates of Pearl, both rich and clear,
And Angels are for Porters there;   90
The Streets thereof transparent gold,
Such as no Eye did e're behold,
A Chrystal River there doth run,
Which doth proceed from the Lambs Throne:
Of Life, there are the waters sure,
Which shall remain for ever pure,

Nor Sun, nor Moon, they have no need,
For glory doth from God proceed:
No Candle there, nor yet Torch light,
For there shall be no darksome night.   100
From sickness and infirmity,
For evermore they shall be free,
Nor withering age shall e're come there,
But beauty shall be bright and clear;
This City pure is not for thee,
For things unclean there shall not be:
If I of Heaven may have my fill,
Take thou the world, and all that will.

The Vanity of all worldly things

As he said vanity, so vain say I,
Oh! vanity, O vain all under Sky;
Where is the man can say, lo I have found
On brittle Earth a Consolation sound?
What is't in honour to be set on high?
No, they like Beasts and Sons of men shall dye:
And whil'st they live, how oft doth turn their fate,
He's now a captive, that was King of late.
What is't in wealth, great Treasures to obtain?
No, that's but labour, anxious care and pain,   10
He heaps up riches, and he heaps up sorrow,
It's his to day, but who's his heir to morrow?
What then? Content in pleasures canst thou find,
More vain than all, that's but to grasp the wind.
The sensual senses for a time they please,
Mean while the conscience rage, who shall appease?
What is't in beauty? No that's but a snare,
They're foul enough to day, that once were fair.

What is't in flowring youth, or manly age?
The first is prone to vice, the last to rage.   20
Where is it then, in wisdom, learning arts?
Sure if on earth, it must be in those parts:
Yet these the wisest man of men did find
But vanity, vexation of mind.
And he that knowes the most, doth still bemoan
He knows not all that here is to be known.
What is it then, to doe as *Stoicks* tell,
Nor laugh, nor weep, let things go ill or well.
Such *Stoicks* are but Stocks such teaching vain,
While man is man, he shall have ease or pain.   30
If not in honour, beauty, age nor treasure,
Nor yet in learning, wisdome, youth nor pleasure,
Where shall I climb, sound, seek, search or find
That *Summum Bonum* which may stay my mind?
There is a path, no vultures eye hath seen,
Where Lion fierce, nor lions whelps have been,
Which leads unto that living Crystal Fount,
Who drinks thereof, the world doth nought account.
The depth and sea have said tis not in me,
With pearl and gold, it shall not valued be.   40
For Saphire, Onix, Topaz who would change:
Its hid from eyes of men, they count it strange.
Death and destruction the fame hath heard,
But where and what it is, from heaven's declar'd,
It brings to honour, which shall ne're decay,
It stores with wealth which time can't wear away.
It yieldeth pleasures far beyond conceit,
And truly beautifies without deceit,
Nor strength, nor wisdome nor fresh youth shall fade
Nor death shall see, but are immortal made.   50
This pearl of price, this tree of life, this spring
Who is possessed of, shall reign a King.

Nor change of state, nor cares shall ever see,
But wear his crown unto eternity:
This satiates the Soul, this stayes the mind,
And all the rest, but Vanity we find.

Davids Lamentation for Saul and Jonathan

2. Sam. 1. 19

Alas slain is the Head of Israel,
Illustrious *Saul* whose beauty did excell,
Upon thy places mountainous and high,
How did the Mighty fall, and falling dye?
In *Gath* let not this thing be spoken on,
Nor published in streets of *Askalon*,
Lest daughters of the Philistines rejoyce,
Lest the uncircumcis'd lift up their voice.
O *Gilbo* Mounts, let never pearled dew,
Nor fruitfull showres your barren tops bestrew,   10
Nor fields of offrings ever on you grow,
Nor any pleasant thing e're may you show;
For there the Mighty Ones did soon decay,
The shield of *Saul* was vilely cast away,
There had his dignity so sore a foyle,
As if his head ne're felt the sacred oyle.
Sometimes from crimson, blood of gastly slain,
The bow of *Jonathan* ne're turn'd in vain:
Nor from the fat, and spoils of Mighty men
With bloodless sword did *Saul* turn back agen.   20
Pleasant and lovely, were they both in life,
And in their death was found no parting strife.
Swifter than swiftest Eagles so were they,
Stronger than Lions ramping for their prey.

O Israels Dames, o'reflow your beauteous eyes
For valiant *Saul* who on Mount *Gilbo* lyes,
Who cloathed you in Cloath of richest Dye,
And choice delights, full of variety,
On your array put ornaments of gold,
Which made you yet more beauteous to behold.   30
O! how in Battle did the mighty fall
In midst of strength not succoured at all.
O lovely *Jonathan*! how wast thou slain?
In places high, full low thou didst remain.
Distrest for thee I am, dear *Jonathan*,
Thy love was wonderfull, surpassing man,
Exceeding all the love that's Feminine,
So pleasant hast thou been, dear brother mine:
How are the mighty fall'n into decay,
And warlike weapons perished away.   40

A Dialogue between Old England and New; concerning their present Troubles, Anno, 1642

New-England

Alas dear Mother, fairest Queen and best,
With honour, wealth, and peace, happy and blest;
What ails thee hang thy head, and cross thine arms?
And sit i'th' dust, to sigh these sad alarms?
What deluge of new woes thus over-whelme
The glories of thy ever famous Realme?
What means this wailing tone, this mournful guise?
Ah, tell thy daughter, she may sympathize.

Old England

Art ignorant indeed of these my woes?
Or must my forced tongue these griefs disclose?   10

And must myself dissect my tatter'd state,
Which 'mazed Christendome stands wondring at?
And thou a Child, a Limbe, and dost not feel
My fainting weakned body now to reel?
This Physick purging potion, I have taken,
Will bring consumption, or an Ague quaking,
Unless some Cordial, thou fetch from high,
Which present help may ease my malady.
If I decease, dost think thou shalt survive?
Or by my wasting state dost think to thrive?   20
Then weigh our case, if't be not justly sad;
Let me lament alone, while thou art glad.

New-England

And thus (alas) your state you much deplore
In general terms, but will not say wherefore:
What medicine shall I seek to cure this woe,
If th' wound's so dangerous I may not know.
But you perhaps, would have me ghess it out:
What hath some *Hengist* like that *Saxon* stout
By fraud or force usurp'd thy flowring crown,
Or by tempestuous warrs thy fields trod down?   30
Or hath *Canutus*, that brave valiant *Dane*
The Regal peacefull Scepter from thee tane?
Or is't a *Norman*, whose victorious hand
With English blood bedews thy conquered land?
Or is't Intestine warrs that thus offend?
Do *Maud* and *Stephen* for the crown contend?
Do Barons rise and side against their King,
And call in foraign aid to help the thing?
Must *Edward* be depos'd? or is't the hour
That second *Richard* must be clapt i'th tower?   40
Or is't the fatal jarre, again begun

That from the red white pricking roses sprung?
Must *Richmonds* aid, the Nobles now implore?
To come and break the Tushes of the Boar,
If none of these dear Mother, what's your woe?
Pray do you fear *Spains* bragging *Armado*?
Doth your Allye, fair *France*, conspire your wrack,
Or do the *Scots* play false, behind your back?
Doth *Holland* quit you ill for all your love?
Whence is the storm from Earth or Heaven above?   50
Is't drought, is't famine, or is't pestilence?
Dost feel the smart, or fear the Consequence?
Your humble Child intreats you, shew your grief,
Though Arms, nor Purse she hath for your relief,
Such is her poverty: yet shall be found
A Suppliant for your help, as she is bound.

Old England

I must confess some of those sores you name,
My beauteous body at this present maime;
But forreign foe, nor feigned friend I fear,   59
For they have work enough (thou knowst) elsewhere
Nor is it *Alcies* Son, nor *Henryes* daughter;
Whose proud contention cause this slaughter,
Nor Nobles siding, to make *John* no King,
French Lewis unjustly to the Crown to bring;
No *Edward*, *Richard*, to lose rule and life,
Nor no *Lancastrians* to renew old strife:
No Duke of *York*, nor Earl of *March* to soyle
Their hands in kindreds blood whom they did foil
No crafty Tyrant now usurps the Seat,
Who Nephews slew that so he might be great;   70
No need of *Tudor*, Roses to unite,
None knows which is the red, or which the white;

Spains braving Fleet, a second time is sunk,
France knows how oft my fury she hath drunk:
By *Edward* third, and *Henry* fifth of fame,
Her Lillies in mine Arms avouch the same.
My Sister *Scotland* hurts me now no more,
Though she hath been injurious heretofore;
What *Holland* is I am in some suspence?
But trust not much unto his excellence.   80
For wants, sure some I feel, but more I fear,
And for the Pestilence, who knows how near;
Famine and Plague, two Sisters of the Sword,
Destruction to a Land, doth soon afford:
They're for my punishment ordain'd on high,
Unless our tears prevent it speedily.
But yet I Answer not what you demand,
To shew the grievance of my troubled Land?
Before I tell th' Effect, I'le shew the Cause
Which are my sins the breach of sacred Laws,   90
Idolatry supplanter of a Nation,
With foolish Superstitious Adoration,
Are lik'd and countenanc'd by men of might,
The Gospel troden down and hath no right:
Church Offices were sold and bought for gain,
That Pope had hope to find, *Rome* here again,
For Oaths and Blasphemies, did ever Ear,
From *Belzebub* himself such language hear;
What scorning of the Saints of the most high?
What injuries did daily on them lye?   100
What false reports, what nick-names did they take
Not for their own, but for their Masters sake?
And thou poor soul, wert jeer'd among the rest,
Thy flying for the truth was made a jest.
For Sabbath-breaking, and for drunkenness,
Did ever land profaness more express?

From crying blood yet cleansed am not I,
Martyres and others, dying causelesly.
How many princely heads on blocks laid down
For nought but title to a fading crown?   110
'Mongst all the crueltyes by great ones done
Oh *Edwards* youths, and *Clarence* hapless son,
O *Jane* why didst thou dye in flowring prime?
Because of royal stem, that was thy crime.
For bribery Adultery and lyes,
Where is the nation, I can't parallize.
With usury, extortion and oppression,
These be the *Hydraes* of my stout transgression.
These be the bitter fountains, heads and roots,   119
Whence flow'd the source, the sprigs, the boughs and fruits
Of more than thou canst hear or I relate,
That with high hand I still did perpetrate:
For these were threatned the wofull day,
I mockt the Preachers, put it far away;
The Sermons yet upon Record do stand
That cri'd destruction to my wicked land:
I then believ'd not, now I feel and see,
The plague of stubborn incredulity.
Some lost their livings, some in prison pent,
Some fin'd, from house and friends to exile went.   130
Their silent tongues to heaven did vengeance cry,
Who saw their wrongs, and hath judg'd righteously
And will repay it seven-fold in my lap:
This is fore-runner of my Afterclap.
Nor took I warning by my neighbours falls,
I saw sad *Germanyes* dismantled walls,
I saw her people famish'd, Nobles slain,
Her fruitfull land, a barren Heath remain.
I saw unmov'd, her Armyes foil'd and fled,
Wives forc'd, babes toss'd, her houses calcined.   140

I saw strong *Rochel* yielded to her Foe,
Thousands of starved Christians there also.
I saw poor *Ireland* bleeding out her last,
Such crueltyes as all reports have past;
Mine heart obdurate stood not yet agast.
Now sip I of that cup, and just't may be
The bottome dreggs reserved are for me.

New-England

To all you've said, sad Mother I assent,
Your fearfull sins great cause there's to lament,
My guilty hands in part, hold up with you,   150
A Sharer in your punishment's my due.
But all you say amounts to this effect,
Not what you feel, but what you do expect,
Pray in plain terms, what is your present grief?
Then let's joyn heads and hearts for your relief.

Old England

Well to the matter then, there's grown of late
'Twixt King and Peers a Question of State,
Which is the chief, the Law, or else the King.
One said, it's he, the other no such thing.
'Tis said, my beter part in Parliament   160
To ease my groaning Land, shew'd their intent,
To crush the proud, and right to each man deal,
To help the Church, and stay the Common-weal.
So many Obstacles came in their way,
As puts me to a stand what I should say;
Old customes, new Prerogatives stood on,
Had they not held Law fast, all had been gone:

Which by their prudence stood them in such stead
They took high *Strafford* lower by the head.
And to their *Laud* be't spoke, they held i'th tower   170
All *Englands* Metropolitane that hour;
This done, an act they would have passed fain,
No Prelate should his Bishoprick retain;
Here tugg'd they hard (indeed,) for all men saw
This must be done by Gospel, not by Law.
Next the Militia they urged sore,
This was deny'd, (I need not say wherefore)
The King displeas'd at *York*, himself absents,
They humbly beg return, shew their intents;
The writing, printing, posting too and fro,   180
Shews all was done, I'le therefore let it go.
But now I come to speak of my disaster,
Contention grown, 'twixt Subjects and their Master;
They worded it so long, they fell to blows,
That thousands lay on heaps, here bleeds my woes,
I that no wars so many years have known,
Am now destroy'd and slaught'red by mine own;
But could the Field alone this strife decide,
One Battel two or three I might abide:
But these may be beginnings of more woe   190
Who knows, but this may be my overthrow.
Oh pity me in this sad perturbation,
My plundred Towns, my houses devastation,
My weeping Virgins and my young men slain;
My wealthy trading fall'n, my dearth of grain,
The seed-times come, but ploughman hath no hope
Because he knows not who shall inn his Crop:
The poor they want their pay, their children bread,
Their woful Mothers tears unpittied,
If any pity in thy heart remain,   200
Or any child-like love thou dost retain,

For my relief, do what there lyes in thee,
And recompence that good I've done to thee.

New England

Dear Mother cease complaints and wipe your eyes,
Shake off your dust, chear up, and now arise,
You are my Mother Nurse, and I your flesh,
Your sunken bowels gladly would refresh,
Your griefs I pity, but soon hope to see,
Out of your troubles much good fruit to be;
To see those latter dayes of hop'd for good,   210
Though now beclouded all with tears and blood:
After dark Popery the day did clear,
But now the Sun in's brightness shall appear.
Blest be the Nobles of thy noble Land,
With ventur'd lives for Truths defence that stand.
Blest be thy Commons, who for common good,
And thy infringed Laws have boldly stood.
Blest be thy Counties, who did aid thee still,
With hearts and States to testifie their will.
Blest be thy Preachers, who do chear thee on,   220
O cry the Sword of God, and *Gideon*;
And shall I not on them wish *Mero*'s curse,
That help thee not with prayers, Arms and purse?
And for my self let miseries abound,
If mindless of thy State I e're be found.
These are the dayes the Churches foes to crush,
To root out Popelings head, tail, branch and rush;
Let's bring *Baals* vestments forth to make a fire,
Their Mytires, Surplices, and all their Tire,
Copes, Rotchets, Crossiers, and such empty trash,   230
And let their Names consume, but let the flash
Light Christendome, and all the world to see
We hate *Romes* whore, with all her trumpery.

Go on brave *Essex* with a Loyal heart,
Not false to King, nor to the better part;
But those that hurt his people and his Crown,
As duty binds, expel and tread them down.
And ye brave Nobles chase away all fear,
And to this hopeful Cause closely adhere;
O Mother can you weep, and have such Peers,   240
When they are gone, then drown your self in tears
If now you weep so much, that then no more
The briny Ocean will o'reflow your shore.
These, these are they I trust, with *Charles* our King,
Out of all mists such glorious dayes shall bring;
That dazled eyes beholding much shall wonder
At that thy setled peace, thy wealth and splendor.
Thy Church and weal establish'd in such manner,
That all shall joy, that thou display'dst thy Banner;
And discipline erected so I trust,   250
That nursing Kings shall come and lick thy dust:
Then Justice shall in all thy Courts take place,
Without respect of person, or of case;
Then Bribes shall cease, and Suits shall not stick long
Patience and purse of Clients oft to wrong:
Then high Commissions shall fall to decay,
And pursivants, and Catchpoles want their pay.
So shall thy happy Nation ever flourish,
When truth and righteousnes they thus shall nourish;
When thus in peace, thine Armies brave send out,   260
To sack proud *Rome*, and all her Vassals rout;
There let thy Name, thy fame, and glory shine,
As did thine Ancestors in *Palestine*:
And let her spoyls full pay, with Interest be,
Of what unjustly once she poll'd from thee.
Of all the woes thou canst, let her be sped,
And on her pour the vengeance threatned;

Bring forth the Beast that rul'd the World with's beck,
And tear his flesh, and set your feet on's neck;
And make his filthy Den so desolate,   270
To th' stonishment of all that knew his state:
This done with brandish'd Swords to *Turky* goe,
For then what is't, but English blades dare do,
And lay her waste for so's the sacred Doom,
And do to *Gog* as thou hast done to *Rome*.
Oh *Abraham*'s seed lift up your heads on high,
For sure the day of your Redemption's nigh;
The Scales shall fall from your long blinded eyes,
And him you shall adore who now despise,
Then fulness of the Nations in shall flow,   280
And Jew and Gentile to one worship go;
Then follows dayes of happiness and rest;
Whose lot doth fall, to live therein is blest:
No Canaanite shall then be found i'th' Land,
And holiness on horses bells shall stand.
If this make way thereto, then sigh no more,
But if at all, thou didst not see't before;
Farewel dear Mother, rightest cause prevail,
And in a while, you'le tell another tale.

VI / FORMAL ELEGIES

*In Honour of that High and Mighty Princess
Queen Elizabeth of happy memory*

The Proeme

Although great Queen thou now in silence lye
Yet thy loud Herald Fame doth to the sky
Thy wondrous worth proclaim in every Clime,
And so hath vow'd while there is world or time.
So great's thy glory and thine excellence,
The sound thereof rapts every humane sence,
That men account it no impiety,
To say thou wert a fleshly Diety:
Thousands bring offerings (though out of date)
Thy world of honours to accumulate,   10
'Mongst hundred Hecatombs of roaring verse,
Mine bleating stands before thy royal Herse.
Thou never didst nor canst thou now disdain
T' accept the tribute of a loyal brain.
Thy clemency did yerst esteem as much
The acclamations of the poor as rich,
Which makes me deem my rudeness is no wrong,
Though I resound thy praises 'mongst the throng.

The Poem

No *Phœnix* pen, nor *Spencers* poetry,
No *Speeds* nor *Cambdens* learned History,   20
Elizahs works, warrs, praise, can e're compact,
The World's the Theatre where she did act.
No memoryes nor volumes can contain
The 'leven Olympiads of her happy reign:

Who was so good, so just, so learn'd so wise,
From all the Kings on earth she won the prize.
Nor say I more than duly is her due,
Millions will testifie that this is true.
She hath wip'd off th' aspersion of her Sex,
That women wisdome lack to play the Rex: 30
Spains Monarch, sayes not so, nor yet his host:
She taught them better manners, to their cost.
The *Salique* law, in force now had not been,
If *France* had ever hop'd for such a Queen.
But can you Doctors now this point dispute,
She's Argument enough to make you mute.
Since first the sun did run his nere run race,
And earth had once a year, a new old face,
Since time was time, and man unmanly man,
Come shew me such a *Phœnix* if you can?   40
Was ever people better rul'd than hers?
Was ever land more happy freed from stirrs?
Did ever wealth in *England* more abound?
Her victoryes in forreign Coasts resound,
Ships more invincible than *Spain*'s, her foe
She wrackt, she sackt, she sunk his Armado:
Her stately troops advanc'd to *Lisbons* wall
Don Anthony in's right there to install.
She frankly helpt, *Franks* brave distressed King,
The States united now her fame do sing,   50
She their Protectrix was, they well do know
Unto our dread Virago, what they owe.
Her Nobles sacrific'd their noble blood,
Nor men nor Coyn she spar'd to do them good.
The rude untamed *Irish*, she did quel,
Before her picture the proud *Tyrone* fell.
Had ever prince such Counsellours as she?
Her self *Minerva* caus'd them so to be.

Such Captains and such souldiers never seen,
As were the Subjects of our *Pallas* Queen.   60
Her Sea-men through all straights the world did round;
Terra incognita might know the sound.
Her *Drake* came laden home with Spanish gold:
Her *Essex* took *Cades*, their Herculean Hold:
But time would fail me, so my tongue would to,
To tell of half she did, or she could doe.
Semiramis to her, is but obscure,
More infamy than fame, she did procure.
She built her glory but on *Babels* walls,
Worlds wonder for a while, but yet it falls.   70
Fierce *Tomris*, (*Cyrus* heads-man) *Scythians* queen,
Had put her harness off, had shee but seen
Our Amazon in th' Camp of *Tilbury*,
Judging all valour and all Majesty
Within that Princess to have residence,
And prostrate yielded to her excellence.
Dido first Foundress of proud *Carthage* walls,
(Who living consummates her Funeralls)
A great *Eliza*, but compar'd with ours,
How vanisheth her glory, wealth and powers.   80
Profuse, proud *Cleopatra*, whose wrong name,
Instead of glory, prov'd her Countryes shame:
Of her what worth in Storyes to be seen,
But that she was a rich Egyptian Queen.
Zenobya potent Empress of the East,
And of all these, without compare the best,
Whom none but great *Aurelius* could quel;
Yet for our Queen is no fit Parallel.
She was a Phœnix Queen, so shall she be,
Her ashes not reviv'd, more Phœnix she.   90
Her personal perfections, who would tell,
Must dip his pen in th' *Heleconian Well*,

Which I may not, my pride doth but aspire
To read what others write, and so admire.
Now say, have women worth? or have they none?
Or had they some, but with our Queen is't gone?
Nay Masculines, you have thus taxt us long,
But she, though dead, will vindicate our wrong.
Let such as say our Sex is void of Reason,
Know tis a Slander now, but once was Treason.   100
But happy *England* which had such a Queen;
Yea happy, happy, had those dayes still been:
But happiness lyes in a higher sphere,
Then wonder not *Eliza* moves not here.
Full fraught with honour, riches and with dayes
She set, she set, like *Titan* in his rayes.
No more shall rise or set so glorious sun
Untill the heavens great revolution,
If then new things their old forms shall retain,
Eliza shall rule *Albion* once again.   110

Her Epitaph

Here sleeps the Queen, this is the Royal Bed,
Of th' Damask Rose, sprung from the white and red,
Whose sweet perfume fills the all-filling Air:
This Rose is wither'd, once so lovely fair.
On neither tree did grow such Rose before,
The greater was our gain, our loss the more.

Another

Here lyes the pride of Queens, Pattern of Kings,
So blaze it Fame, here's feathers for thy wings.
Here lyes the envi'd, yet unparalled Prince,
Whose living virtues speak, (though dead long since)   120
If many worlds, as that Fantastick fram'd,
In every one be her great glory fam'd.

An Elegie upon that Honourable and renowned Knight Sir Philip Sidney, who was untimely slain at the Siege of Zutphen, Anno, 1.586

When *England* did enjoy her Halsion dayes,
Her noble *Sidney* wore the Crown of Bayes;
As well an honour to our *British* Land,
As she that sway'd the Scepter with her hand;
Mars and *Minerva* did in one agree,
Of Arms and Arts he should a pattern be,
Calliope with *Terpsichore* did sing,
Of Poesie, and of musick, he was King;
His Rhetorick struck *Polimina* dead,
His Eloquence made *Mercury* wax red;   10
His *Logick* from *Euterpe* won the Crown,
More worth was his than *Clio* could set down.
Thalia and *Melpomene* say truth,
(Witness *Arcadia* penned in his youth,)
Are not his tragick Comedies so acted,
As if your ninefold wit had been compacted.
To shew the world, they never saw before,
That this one Volume should exhaust your store;
His wiser dayes condemn'd his witty works,
Who knows the spels that in his Rhetorick lurks,   20
But some infatuate fools soon caught therein,
Fond *Cupids* Dame had never such a gin,
Which makes severer eyes but slight that story,
And men of morose minds envy his glory:
But he's a Beetle-head that can't descry
A world of wealth within that rubbish lye,
And doth his name, his work, his honour wrong,
The brave refiner of our British tongue,
That sees not learning, valour and morality,
Justice, friendship, and kind hospitality,   30

Yea and Divinity within his book,
Such were prejudicate, and did not look.
In all Records his name I ever see
Put with an Epithite of dignity,
Which shews his worth was great, his honour such,
The love his Country ought him, was as much.
Then let none disallow of these my straines
Whilst English blood yet runs within my veins.
O brave *Achilles*, I wish some *Homer* would
Engrave in Marble, with Characters of gold   40
The valiant feats thou didst on *Flanders* coast,
Which at this day fair *Belgia* may boast.
The more I say, the more thy worth I stain,
Thy fame and praise is far beyond my strain.
O *Zutphen*, *Zutphen* that most fatal City
Made famous by thy death, much more the pity:
Ah! in his blooming prime death pluckt this rose
E're he was ripe, his thread cut *Atropos*.
Thus man is born to dye, and dead is he,
Brave *Hector*, by the walls of *Troy* we see.   50
O who was near thee but did sore repine
He rescued not with life that life of thine:
But yet impartial Fates this boon did give,
Though *Sidney* di'd his valiant name should live:
And live it doth in spight of death through fame,
Thus being overcome, he overcame.
Where is that envious tongue, but can afford
Of this our noble *Scipio* some good word.
Great *Bartas* this unto thy praise adds more,
In sad sweet verse, thou didst his death deplore.   60
And *Phœnix Spencer* doth unto his life,
His death present in sable to his wife.
Stella the fair, whose streams from Conduits fell
For the sad loss of her dear *Astrophel*.

Fain would I shew how he fames paths did tread,
But now into such Lab'rinths I am lead,
With endless turnes, the way I find not out,
How to persist my Muse is more in doubt;
Which makes me now with *Silvester* confess,
But *Sidney*'s Muse can sing his worthiness.   70
The Muses aid I crav'd, they had no will
To give to their Detractor any quill,
With high disdain, they said they gave no more,
Since *Sidney* had exhausted all their store.
They took from me the scribling pen I had,
(I to be eas'd of such a task was glad)
Then to reveng this wrong, themselves engage,
And drave me from *Parnassus* in a rage.
Then wonder not if I no better sped,
Since I the Muses thus have injured.   80
I pensive for my fault, sate down, and then
Errata through their leave, threw me my pen,
My Poem to conclude, two lines they deign
Which writ, she bad return't to them again;
So *Sidneys* fame I leave to *Englands* Rolls,
His bones do lie interr'd in stately *Pauls*.

His Epitaph

Here lies in fame under this stone,
Philip and *Alexander* both in one;
Heir to the Muses, the Son of *Mars* in Truth,
Learning, Valour, Wisdome, all in virtuous youth,   90
His praise is much, this shall suffice my pen,
That *Sidney* dy'd 'mong most renown'd of men.

To her most Honoured Father Thomas Dudley Esq;
these humbly presented

Dear Sir of late delighted with the sight
Of your four Sisters cloth'd in black and white,
Of fairer Dames the Sun, ne'r saw the face;
Though made a pedestal for *Adams* Race;
Their worth so shines in these rich lines you show
Their paralels to finde I scarcely know
To climbe their Climes, I have nor strength nor skill
To mount so high requires an Eagles quill;
Yet view thereof did cause my thoughts to soar;
My lowly pen might wait upon these four,   10
I bring my four times four, now meanly clad
To do their homage, unto yours, full glad:
Who for their Age, their worth and quality
Might seem of yours to claim precedency:
But by my humble hand, thus rudely pen'd
They are, your bounden handmaids to attend.
These same are they, from whom we being have,
These are of all, the Life, the Nurse, the Grave,
These are the hot, the cold, the moist, the dry,
That sink, that swim, that fill, that upwards fly,   20
Of these consists our bodies, Cloathes and Food,
The World, the useful, hurtful, and the good,
Sweet harmony they keep, yet jar oft times
Their discord doth appear, by these harsh rimes.
Yours did contest for wealth, for Arts, for Age,
My first do shew their good, and then their rage.
My other foures do intermixed tell
Each others faults, and where themselves excell;
How hot and dry contend with moist and cold,
How Air and Earth no correspondence hold,   30

And yet in equal tempers, how they 'gree
How divers natures make one Unity
Something of all (though mean) I did intend
But fear'd you'ld judge *Du Bartas* was my friend,
I honour him, but dare not wear his wealth
My goods are true (though poor) I love no stealth
But if I did I durst not send them you
Who must reward a Thief, but with his due.
I shall not need, mine innocence to clear
These ragged lines, will do't, when they appear: 40
On what they are, your mild aspect I crave
Accept my best, my worst vouchsafe a Grave.

From her that to your self, more duty owes
Than water in the boundlesse Ocean flows.

The Prologue

1

To sing of Wars, of Captains, and of Kings,
Of Cities founded, Common-wealths begun,
For my mean pen are too superiour things:
Or how they all, or each their dates have run
Let Poets and Historians set these forth,
My obscure Lines shall not so dim their worth.

2

But when my wondring eyes and envious heart
Great *Bartas* sugar'd lines, do but read o're
Fool I do grudg the Muses did not part
'Twixt him and me that overfluent store;
A *Bartas* can, do what a *Bartas* will
But simple I according to my skill. 12

3

From school-boyes tongue no rhet'rick we expect
Nor yet a sweet Consort from broken strings,
Nor perfect beauty, where's a main defect:
My foolish, broken, blemish'd Muse so sings
And this to mend, alas, no Art is able,
'Cause nature, made it so irreparable.

4

Nor can I, like that fluent sweet tongu'd Greek,
Who lisp'd at first, in future times speak plain
By Art he gladly found what he did seek
A full requital of his striving paine:
Art can do much, but this maxime's most sure
A weak or wounded brain admits no cure.   24

5

I am obnoxious to each carping tongue
Who says my hand a needle better fits,
A Poets pen all scorn I should thus wrong,
For such despite they cast on Female wits:
If what I do prove well, it won't advance,
They'l say it's stoln, or else it was by chance.

6

But sure the Antique Greeks were far more mild
Else of our Sexe, why feigned they those Nine
And poesy made, *Calliope's* own Child;
So 'mongst the rest they placed the Arts Divine,
But this weak knot, they will full soon untie,
The Greeks did nought, but play the fools and lye.   36

7

Let Greeks be Greeks, and women what they are
Men have precedency and still excell,
It is but vain unjustly to wage warre;
Men can do best, and women know it well
Preheminence in all and each is yours;
Yet grant some small acknowledgement of ours.

8

And oh ye high flown quills that soar the Skies,
And ever with your prey still catch your praise,
If e're you daigne these lowly lines your eyes
Give Thyme or Parsley wreath, I ask no bayes,
This mean and unrefined ure of mine
Will make your glistering gold but more to shine.   48